50 Tempura Lover's Cookbook Recipes

By: Kelly Johnson

Table of Contents

- Classic Shrimp Tempura
- Vegetable Tempura (Assorted)
- Sweet Potato Tempura
- Eggplant Tempura
- Zucchini Tempura
- Bell Pepper Tempura
- Broccoli Tempura
- Onion Ring Tempura
- Mushroom Tempura (Shiitake and Enoki)
- Green Bean Tempura
- Asparagus Tempura
- Pumpkin Tempura
- Cauliflower Tempura
- Squash Tempura
- Tofu Tempura
- Avocado Tempura
- Seaweed Tempura (Nori)
- Lotus Root Tempura
- Tempura Fish (White Fish)
- Tempura Calamari
- Tempura Scallops
- Tempura Lobster
- Tempura Soft Shell Crab
- Tempura Chicken
- Tempura with Dipping Sauce (Tentsuyu)
- Tempura Udon (Noodles)
- Tempura Rice Bowl
- Tempura Sushi Rolls
- Spicy Tempura Shrimp Tacos
- Tempura Salad with Sesame Dressing
- Tempura Soba Noodles
- Tempura Donburi (Rice Bowl)
- Tempura Vegetable Platter
- Tempura with Ponzu Sauce
- Sweet Tempura (Sugar Coated)

- Tempura Fritters (Mixed Veggies)
- Matcha Tempura
- Tempura Cheesecake Bites
- Tempura Fruit (Banana, Apple)
- Tempura Spring Rolls
- Kimchi Tempura
- Garlic Tempura
- Tempura Panko-Crusted Shrimp
- Tempura with Miso Glaze
- Spicy Tuna Tempura Roll
- Tempura Hotpot
- Tempura Banh Mi Sandwich
- Churros Tempura
- Cream Cheese Tempura
- Chocolate Tempura Brownies

Classic Shrimp Tempura

Ingredients:

- 10 large shrimp, peeled and deveined
- 1 cup all-purpose flour
- 1/2 cup cornstarch
- 1 cup ice-cold water
- 1 egg, lightly beaten
- Oil for frying

Instructions:

1. In a bowl, mix flour and cornstarch.
2. In another bowl, combine ice-cold water and egg.
3. Dip shrimp into the flour mixture, then into the batter.
4. Heat oil in a deep pan and fry shrimp until golden brown. Drain on paper towels.

Vegetable Tempura (Assorted)

Ingredients:

- 1 cup assorted vegetables (carrots, sweet potatoes, zucchini, bell peppers)
- 1 cup all-purpose flour
- 1/2 cup cornstarch
- 1 cup ice-cold water
- 1 egg, lightly beaten
- Oil for frying

Instructions:

1. Prepare vegetables by slicing them into thin pieces.
2. Mix flour and cornstarch in a bowl.
3. In another bowl, combine ice-cold water and egg.
4. Dip vegetables into the flour mixture, then into the batter.
5. Fry in hot oil until crispy and golden. Drain on paper towels.

Sweet Potato Tempura

Ingredients:

- 1 medium sweet potato, sliced into thin rounds
- 1 cup all-purpose flour
- 1/2 cup cornstarch
- 1 cup ice-cold water
- 1 egg, lightly beaten
- Oil for frying

Instructions:

1. Mix flour and cornstarch in a bowl.
2. In another bowl, combine ice-cold water and egg.
3. Dip sweet potato slices into the flour mixture, then into the batter.
4. Fry in hot oil until golden brown. Drain on paper towels.

Eggplant Tempura

Ingredients:

- 1 medium eggplant, sliced into thin rounds
- 1 cup all-purpose flour
- 1/2 cup cornstarch
- 1 cup ice-cold water
- 1 egg, lightly beaten
- Oil for frying

Instructions:

1. Mix flour and cornstarch in a bowl.
2. In another bowl, combine ice-cold water and egg.
3. Dip eggplant slices into the flour mixture, then into the batter.
4. Fry in hot oil until crispy and golden. Drain on paper towels.

Zucchini Tempura

Ingredients:

- 1 medium zucchini, sliced into thin rounds
- 1 cup all-purpose flour
- 1/2 cup cornstarch
- 1 cup ice-cold water
- 1 egg, lightly beaten
- Oil for frying

Instructions:

1. Mix flour and cornstarch in a bowl.
2. In another bowl, combine ice-cold water and egg.
3. Dip zucchini slices into the flour mixture, then into the batter.
4. Fry in hot oil until crispy and golden. Drain on paper towels.

Bell Pepper Tempura

Ingredients:

- 1 bell pepper, sliced into thin strips
- 1 cup all-purpose flour
- 1/2 cup cornstarch
- 1 cup ice-cold water
- 1 egg, lightly beaten
- Oil for frying

Instructions:

1. Mix flour and cornstarch in a bowl.
2. In another bowl, combine ice-cold water and egg.
3. Dip bell pepper strips into the flour mixture, then into the batter.
4. Fry in hot oil until crispy and golden. Drain on paper towels.

Broccoli Tempura

Ingredients:

- 1 cup broccoli florets
- 1 cup all-purpose flour
- 1/2 cup cornstarch
- 1 cup ice-cold water
- 1 egg, lightly beaten
- Oil for frying

Instructions:

1. Mix flour and cornstarch in a bowl.
2. In another bowl, combine ice-cold water and egg.
3. Dip broccoli florets into the flour mixture, then into the batter.
4. Fry in hot oil until crispy and golden. Drain on paper towels.

Onion Ring Tempura

Ingredients:

- 1 large onion, sliced into rings
- 1 cup all-purpose flour
- 1/2 cup cornstarch
- 1 cup ice-cold water
- 1 egg, lightly beaten
- Oil for frying

Instructions:
1. Mix flour and cornstarch in a bowl.
2. In another bowl, combine ice-cold water and egg.
3. Dip onion rings into the flour mixture, then into the batter.
4. Fry in hot oil until crispy and golden. Drain on paper towels.

Mushroom Tempura (Shiitake and Enoki)

Ingredients:

- 1 cup shiitake mushrooms, stemmed
- 1 cup enoki mushrooms, trimmed
- 1 cup all-purpose flour
- 1/2 cup cornstarch
- 1 cup ice-cold water
- 1 egg, lightly beaten
- Oil for frying

Instructions:

1. Mix flour and cornstarch in a bowl.
2. In another bowl, combine ice-cold water and egg.
3. Dip mushrooms into the flour mixture, then into the batter.
4. Fry in hot oil until crispy and golden. Drain on paper towels.

Green Bean Tempura

Ingredients:

- 1 cup green beans, trimmed
- 1 cup all-purpose flour
- 1/2 cup cornstarch
- 1 cup ice-cold water
- 1 egg, lightly beaten
- Oil for frying

Instructions:

1. Mix flour and cornstarch in a bowl.
2. In another bowl, combine ice-cold water and egg.
3. Dip green beans into the flour mixture, then into the batter.
4. Fry in hot oil until crispy and golden. Drain on paper towels.

Asparagus Tempura

Ingredients:

- 1 bunch asparagus, trimmed
- 1 cup all-purpose flour
- 1/2 cup cornstarch
- 1 cup ice-cold water
- 1 egg, lightly beaten
- Oil for frying

Instructions:

1. Mix flour and cornstarch in a bowl.
2. In another bowl, combine ice-cold water and egg.
3. Dip asparagus into the flour mixture, then into the batter.
4. Fry in hot oil until crispy and golden. Drain on paper towels.

Pumpkin Tempura

Ingredients:

- 1 cup pumpkin, sliced into thin pieces
- 1 cup all-purpose flour
- 1/2 cup cornstarch
- 1 cup ice-cold water
- 1 egg, lightly beaten
- Oil for frying

Instructions:

1. Mix flour and cornstarch in a bowl.
2. In another bowl, combine ice-cold water and egg.
3. Dip pumpkin slices into the flour mixture, then into the batter.
4. Fry in hot oil until crispy and golden. Drain on paper towels.

Cauliflower Tempura

Ingredients:

- 1 cup cauliflower florets
- 1 cup all-purpose flour
- 1/2 cup cornstarch
- 1 cup ice-cold water
- 1 egg, lightly beaten
- Oil for frying

Instructions:

1. Mix flour and cornstarch in a bowl.
2. In another bowl, combine ice-cold water and egg.
3. Dip cauliflower florets into the flour mixture, then into the batter.
4. Fry in hot oil until crispy and golden. Drain on paper towels.

Squash Tempura

Ingredients:

- 1 cup squash, sliced into thin pieces
- 1 cup all-purpose flour
- 1/2 cup cornstarch
- 1 cup ice-cold water
- 1 egg, lightly beaten
- Oil for frying

Instructions:

1. Mix flour and cornstarch in a bowl.
2. In another bowl, combine ice-cold water and egg.
3. Dip squash slices into the flour mixture, then into the batter.
4. Fry in hot oil until crispy and golden. Drain on paper towels.

Tofu Tempura

Ingredients:

- 1 block firm tofu, cut into cubes
- 1 cup all-purpose flour
- 1/2 cup cornstarch
- 1 cup ice-cold water
- 1 egg, lightly beaten
- Oil for frying

Instructions:

1. Mix flour and cornstarch in a bowl.
2. In another bowl, combine ice-cold water and egg.
3. Dip tofu cubes into the flour mixture, then into the batter.
4. Fry in hot oil until crispy and golden. Drain on paper towels.

Avocado Tempura

Ingredients:

- 1 ripe avocado, sliced into wedges
- 1 cup all-purpose flour
- 1/2 cup cornstarch
- 1 cup ice-cold water
- 1 egg, lightly beaten
- Oil for frying

Instructions:

1. Mix flour and cornstarch in a bowl.
2. In another bowl, combine ice-cold water and egg.
3. Dip avocado slices into the flour mixture, then into the batter.
4. Fry in hot oil until crispy and golden. Drain on paper towels.

Seaweed Tempura (Nori)

Ingredients:

- 4 sheets nori (seaweed)
- 1 cup all-purpose flour
- 1/2 cup cornstarch
- 1 cup ice-cold water
- 1 egg, lightly beaten
- Oil for frying

Instructions:

1. Cut nori sheets into smaller pieces.
2. Mix flour and cornstarch in a bowl.
3. In another bowl, combine ice-cold water and egg.
4. Dip nori pieces into the flour mixture, then into the batter.
5. Fry in hot oil until crispy and golden. Drain on paper towels.

Lotus Root Tempura

Ingredients:

- 1 cup lotus root, sliced into thin rounds
- 1 cup all-purpose flour
- 1/2 cup cornstarch
- 1 cup ice-cold water
- 1 egg, lightly beaten
- Oil for frying

Instructions:

1. Mix flour and cornstarch in a bowl.
2. In another bowl, combine ice-cold water and egg.
3. Dip lotus root slices into the flour mixture, then into the batter.
4. Fry in hot oil until crispy and golden. Drain on paper towels.

Tempura Fish (White Fish)

Ingredients:

- 1 pound white fish fillets, cut into strips
- 1 cup all-purpose flour
- 1/2 cup cornstarch
- 1 cup ice-cold water
- 1 egg, lightly beaten
- Oil for frying

Instructions:

1. Mix flour and cornstarch in a bowl.
2. In another bowl, combine ice-cold water and egg.
3. Dip fish strips into the flour mixture, then into the batter.
4. Fry in hot oil until crispy and golden. Drain on paper towels.

Tempura Calamari

Ingredients:

- 1 pound calamari, cleaned and sliced into rings
- 1 cup all-purpose flour
- 1/2 cup cornstarch
- 1 cup ice-cold water
- 1 egg, lightly beaten
- Oil for frying

Instructions:

1. Mix flour and cornstarch in a bowl.
2. In another bowl, combine ice-cold water and egg.
3. Dip calamari rings into the flour mixture, then into the batter.
4. Fry in hot oil until crispy and golden. Drain on paper towels.

Tempura Scallops

Ingredients:

- 1 pound scallops, patted dry
- 1 cup all-purpose flour
- 1/2 cup cornstarch
- 1 cup ice-cold water
- 1 egg, lightly beaten
- Oil for frying

Instructions:

1. Mix flour and cornstarch in a bowl.
2. In another bowl, combine ice-cold water and egg.
3. Dip scallops into the flour mixture, then into the batter.
4. Fry in hot oil until crispy and golden. Drain on paper towels.

Tempura Lobster

Ingredients:

- 1 pound lobster tail, cut into bite-sized pieces
- 1 cup all-purpose flour
- 1/2 cup cornstarch
- 1 cup ice-cold water
- 1 egg, lightly beaten
- Oil for frying

Instructions:

1. Mix flour and cornstarch in a bowl.
2. In another bowl, combine ice-cold water and egg.
3. Dip lobster pieces into the flour mixture, then into the batter.
4. Fry in hot oil until crispy and golden. Drain on paper towels.

Tempura Soft Shell Crab

Ingredients:

- 4 soft shell crabs, cleaned
- 1 cup all-purpose flour
- 1/2 cup cornstarch
- 1 cup ice-cold water
- 1 egg, lightly beaten
- Oil for frying

Instructions:
1. Mix flour and cornstarch in a bowl.
2. In another bowl, combine ice-cold water and egg.
3. Dip soft shell crabs into the flour mixture, then into the batter.
4. Fry in hot oil until crispy and golden. Drain on paper towels.

Tempura Chicken

Ingredients:

- 1 pound chicken breast, cut into bite-sized pieces
- 1 cup all-purpose flour
- 1/2 cup cornstarch
- 1 cup ice-cold water
- 1 egg, lightly beaten
- Oil for frying

Instructions:

1. Mix flour and cornstarch in a bowl.
2. In another bowl, combine ice-cold water and egg.
3. Dip chicken pieces into the flour mixture, then into the batter.
4. Fry in hot oil until crispy and golden. Drain on paper towels.

Tempura with Dipping Sauce (Tentsuyu)

Ingredients:

- 1 cup dashi stock
- 1/4 cup soy sauce
- 1/4 cup mirin
- Grated daikon radish (for serving)

Instructions:

1. In a small saucepan, combine dashi, soy sauce, and mirin.
2. Heat gently until warm.
3. Serve with grated daikon on the side.

Tempura Udon

Ingredients:

- 2 servings udon noodles
- Assorted tempura (shrimp, vegetables)
- Dashi broth (prepared)
- Green onions, chopped (for garnish)

Instructions:

1. Cook udon noodles according to package instructions.
2. Heat dashi broth until warm.
3. Divide udon into bowls, pour dashi over noodles, and top with tempura and green onions.

Tempura Rice Bowl

Ingredients:

- Cooked rice (for serving)
- Assorted tempura (shrimp, vegetables)
- Soy sauce or tentsuyu (for drizzling)

Instructions:

1. Place cooked rice in a bowl.
2. Top with assorted tempura.
3. Drizzle with soy sauce or tentsuyu before serving.

Tempura Sushi Rolls

Ingredients:

- Sushi rice (prepared)
- Nori sheets
- Assorted tempura (shrimp, vegetables)
- Soy sauce (for dipping)

Instructions:

1. Lay a nori sheet on a bamboo mat.
2. Spread sushi rice over nori, leaving a border.
3. Place tempura in the center and roll tightly.
4. Slice and serve with soy sauce.

Spicy Tempura Shrimp Tacos

Ingredients:

- Tempura shrimp
- Taco shells
- Spicy mayo (mayonnaise mixed with sriracha)
- Shredded cabbage (for topping)

Instructions:

1. Fill taco shells with tempura shrimp.
2. Drizzle with spicy mayo and top with shredded cabbage.
3. Serve immediately.

Tempura Salad with Sesame Dressing

Ingredients:

- Mixed greens (for salad)
- Assorted tempura (shrimp, vegetables)
- Sesame dressing

Instructions:

1. Arrange mixed greens on a plate.
2. Top with assorted tempura.
3. Drizzle with sesame dressing before serving.

Tempura Soba Noodles

Ingredients:

- 2 servings soba noodles
- Assorted tempura (shrimp, vegetables)
- Soy sauce or tentsuyu (for serving)

Instructions:

1. Cook soba noodles according to package instructions.
2. Drain and rinse under cold water.
3. Serve noodles topped with tempura and a side of soy sauce or tentsuyu.

Tempura Donburi (Rice Bowl)

Ingredients:

- Cooked rice (for serving)
- Assorted tempura (shrimp, vegetables)
- Dashi broth (prepared)
- Egg (optional, for drizzle)

Instructions:

1. Place cooked rice in a bowl.
2. Top with assorted tempura.
3. Pour warm dashi over the top, and drizzle with a beaten egg if desired.

Tempura Vegetable Platter

Ingredients:

- Assorted vegetables (e.g., sweet potatoes, bell peppers, zucchini, broccoli)
- 1 cup all-purpose flour
- 1/2 cup cornstarch
- 1 cup ice-cold water
- 1 egg, lightly beaten
- Oil for frying

Instructions:

1. Cut vegetables into bite-sized pieces.
2. Mix flour and cornstarch in a bowl.
3. In another bowl, combine ice-cold water and egg.
4. Dip vegetables into the flour mixture, then into the batter.
5. Fry in hot oil until crispy and golden. Drain on paper towels.

Tempura with Ponzu Sauce

Ingredients:

- Assorted tempura (shrimp, vegetables)
- 1/2 cup soy sauce
- 1/4 cup citrus juice (yuzu or lemon)
- 1 tablespoon mirin
- Grated daikon radish (for serving)

Instructions:

1. In a bowl, mix soy sauce, citrus juice, and mirin.
2. Serve tempura with ponzu sauce and grated daikon on the side.

Sweet Tempura (Sugar Coated)

Ingredients:

- Assorted sweet items (e.g., banana slices, sweet potato, apple slices)
- 1 cup all-purpose flour
- 1/2 cup cornstarch
- 1 cup ice-cold water
- Oil for frying
- Sugar (for coating)

Instructions:

1. Cut sweet items into bite-sized pieces.
2. Mix flour and cornstarch in a bowl.
3. Dip sweet items into the batter and fry until golden.
4. Coat with sugar while still warm.

Tempura Fritters (Mixed Veggies)

Ingredients:

- Assorted vegetables (e.g., carrots, zucchini, green onions)
- 1 cup all-purpose flour
- 1/2 cup cornstarch
- 1 cup ice-cold water
- 1 egg, lightly beaten
- Oil for frying

Instructions:

1. Chop vegetables into small pieces.
2. Mix flour and cornstarch in a bowl.
3. In another bowl, combine ice-cold water and egg.
4. Mix vegetables into the batter.
5. Fry spoonfuls in hot oil until crispy and golden. Drain on paper towels.

Matcha Tempura

Ingredients:

- Assorted vegetables (e.g., sweet potatoes, zucchini)
- 1 cup all-purpose flour
- 1/2 cup cornstarch
- 1 tablespoon matcha powder
- 1 cup ice-cold water
- 1 egg, lightly beaten
- Oil for frying

Instructions:

1. Mix flour, cornstarch, and matcha in a bowl.
2. In another bowl, combine ice-cold water and egg.
3. Dip vegetables into the batter and fry in hot oil until crispy.
4. Drain on paper towels.

Tempura Cheesecake Bites

Ingredients:

- 8 ounces cheesecake (cut into bite-sized pieces)
- 1 cup all-purpose flour
- 1/2 cup cornstarch
- 1 cup ice-cold water
- 1 egg, lightly beaten
- Oil for frying
- Powdered sugar (for dusting)

Instructions:

1. Freeze cheesecake bites until firm.
2. Mix flour and cornstarch in a bowl.
3. In another bowl, combine ice-cold water and egg.
4. Dip frozen cheesecake bites into the batter and fry until golden.
5. Dust with powdered sugar before serving.

Tempura Fruit (Banana, Apple)

Ingredients:

- 1 banana, sliced
- 1 apple, sliced
- 1 cup all-purpose flour
- 1/2 cup cornstarch
- 1 cup ice-cold water
- Oil for frying
- Sugar (for coating)

Instructions:

1. Cut banana and apple into slices.
2. Mix flour and cornstarch in a bowl.
3. Dip fruit slices into the batter and fry until golden.
4. Coat with sugar while still warm.

Tempura Spring Rolls

Ingredients:

- 4 spring roll wrappers
- Assorted vegetables (e.g., carrots, cabbage, bell peppers)
- 1 cup all-purpose flour
- 1/2 cup cornstarch
- 1 cup ice-cold water
- Oil for frying

Instructions:

1. Fill spring roll wrappers with assorted vegetables and roll tightly.
2. Mix flour and cornstarch in a bowl.
3. Dip spring rolls into the batter and fry until crispy.
4. Drain on paper towels and serve with dipping sauce.

Kimchi Tempura

Ingredients:

- 1 cup kimchi (drained and chopped)
- 1 cup all-purpose flour
- 1/2 cup cornstarch
- 1 cup ice-cold water
- 1 egg, lightly beaten
- Oil for frying

Instructions:

1. Mix flour and cornstarch in a bowl.
2. In another bowl, combine ice-cold water and egg.
3. Dip kimchi pieces into the batter and fry in hot oil until crispy.
4. Drain on paper towels before serving.

Garlic Tempura

Ingredients:

- 1 cup garlic cloves (peeled)
- 1 cup all-purpose flour
- 1/2 cup cornstarch
- 1 cup ice-cold water
- 1 egg, lightly beaten
- Oil for frying

Instructions:

1. Mix flour and cornstarch in a bowl.
2. In another bowl, combine ice-cold water and egg.
3. Dip garlic cloves into the batter and fry until golden and crispy.
4. Drain on paper towels before serving.

Tempura Panko-Crusted Shrimp

Ingredients:

- 1 pound shrimp (peeled and deveined)
- 1 cup panko breadcrumbs
- 1 cup all-purpose flour
- 1/2 cup cornstarch
- 1 cup ice-cold water
- 1 egg, lightly beaten
- Oil for frying

Instructions:

1. Mix flour and cornstarch in a bowl.
2. In another bowl, combine ice-cold water and egg.
3. Dip shrimp into the batter, then coat with panko breadcrumbs.
4. Fry in hot oil until crispy and golden. Drain on paper towels before serving.

Tempura with Miso Glaze

Ingredients:

- Assorted tempura (shrimp, vegetables)
- 1/2 cup miso paste
- 1/4 cup mirin
- 1/4 cup water
- 1 tablespoon sesame oil

Instructions:

1. In a small saucepan, mix miso paste, mirin, water, and sesame oil.
2. Heat gently until smooth and warm.
3. Serve tempura drizzled with miso glaze.

Spicy Tuna Tempura Roll

Ingredients:

- Sushi rice (prepared)
- Nori sheets
- Spicy tuna (tuna mixed with mayo and sriracha)
- Tempura shrimp (cooked)
- Soy sauce (for dipping)

Instructions:

1. Lay a nori sheet on a bamboo mat.
2. Spread sushi rice over nori, leaving a border.
3. Add spicy tuna and tempura shrimp in the center.
4. Roll tightly and slice. Serve with soy sauce.

Tempura Hotpot

Ingredients:

- Assorted tempura (shrimp, vegetables)
- Dashi broth (prepared)
- Sliced mushrooms
- Leafy greens (e.g., spinach, bok choy)
- Tofu (cubed)

Instructions:

1. In a pot, heat dashi broth.
2. Add mushrooms, greens, and tofu.
3. Serve hotpot with assorted tempura on the side.

Tempura Banh Mi Sandwich

Ingredients:

- Baguette
- Assorted tempura (shrimp, vegetables)
- Pickled carrots and daikon
- Fresh cucumber slices
- Cilantro sprigs
- Spicy mayo (for spreading)

Instructions:

1. Slice baguette lengthwise and spread with spicy mayo.
2. Layer with tempura, pickled vegetables, cucumber, and cilantro.
3. Close the sandwich and serve immediately.

Churros Tempura

Ingredients:

- 1 cup churro dough (prepared)
- 1 cup all-purpose flour
- 1/2 cup cornstarch
- 1 cup ice-cold water
- 1 egg, lightly beaten
- Oil for frying
- Sugar (for coating)

Instructions:

1. Prepare churro dough and pipe into desired shapes.
2. Mix flour and cornstarch in a bowl.
3. Dip churros into the batter and fry until golden.
4. Coat with sugar before serving.

Cream Cheese Tempura

Ingredients:

- 8 oz cream cheese (cut into bite-sized pieces)
- 1 cup all-purpose flour
- 1/2 cup cornstarch
- 1 cup ice-cold water
- 1 egg, lightly beaten
- Oil for frying

Instructions:

1. Mix flour and cornstarch in a bowl.
2. In another bowl, combine ice-cold water and egg.
3. Dip cream cheese pieces into the batter and fry in hot oil until golden and crispy.
4. Drain on paper towels before serving.

Chocolate Tempura Brownies

Ingredients:

- 1 batch of brownies (prepared and cooled)
- 1 cup all-purpose flour
- 1/2 cup cornstarch
- 1 cup ice-cold water
- 1 egg, lightly beaten
- Oil for frying
- Powdered sugar (for dusting)

Instructions:

1. Cut cooled brownies into bite-sized squares.
2. Mix flour and cornstarch in a bowl.
3. In another bowl, combine ice-cold water and egg.
4. Dip brownie pieces into the batter and fry in hot oil until crispy.
5. Drain on paper towels and dust with powdered sugar before serving.

www.ingramcontent.com/pod-product-compliance
Lightning Source LLC
LaVergne TN
LVHW081505060526
838201LV00056BA/2944